What to Expect

When You're Dead

by

JOHN FARQUHAR

Hypothetical Press

This book is a work of humor and of fiction. The names, characters, places and incidents are products of the writer's imagination or have been used fictitiously and are not to be construed as real incidents or conversations. No religious organizations, physicists, spiritualists, philosophers, or dead people were consulted in or harmed by the making of this book.

Published by Hypothetical Press
www.hypotheticalpress.com

Cover photo credit: ginasanders / 123RF

ISBN-13:978-0989818902

First Printing September 2013

To all those atheists who have died,
and gone grudgingly to Heaven.

Table of Contents

WHAT TO EXPECT WHEN YOU'RE DEAD

BY JOHN FARQUHAR

Forward

*F*ew, until now, have gone to their grave with a reliable guide book. This is the work you are now holding in your hands, the product of years of research, and painstaking paranormal investigation. There are far too many authors telling you how to live your life on this transient earth, not nearly enough charting the unchanging magnificence that the spirit delights in when, in death, we burn through this shallow shell of a body and shoot into the next world as a boundless beam of pure light. The time is ripe to rectify that deficiency and reveal to you, my fellow Americans, what the government and so-called mainstream religions have hidden from you for far too long: the very nooks and crannies of Eternity.

This is, if I may say, a timely text. Consider the facts: billions and billions of souls have already taken the one-way trip; thousands more will have done so by the time you reach this word. It's getting a little crowded up there; tempers are getting frayed. Some pushing and shoving by Germans has been reported. Now more than ever you need to know in advance what to expect when you're dead. This is the book to satisfy all your curiosity, respond to all your immortal needs. This book has been written to make your journey through the After-Life a positive, dynamic and truly fulfilling experience.

Once you have read it, no corpse will be better informed, more ready to take on the challenge of immortality than yours. In the race to meet your Maker, you will have a significant head start on European Intellectuals, Eastern Mystics, every religious denomination in the world, and the Masons. The journey to God, though, is a marathon, not a sprint. I will take you step by step through every tricky process, every potential pitfall, every potential pit. Starting with infallible tests that you can take to prove that you are in fact dead, I will go on to advise you how to cope with the roller-coaster of emotions you may be feeling; the enormous changes that you undergo, due to having no hormones whatsoever. I'll tell you how to avoid embarrassing pauses when you finally talk to God, give handy hints on spiritual self-esteem to those of a shy and retiring nature.

Even after you've met Your Creator, I won't leave you in the lurch. One of the many ground-breaking discoveries in this book is that many dead people, after they've met God and achieved what they thought was their Ultimate Goal, fall prey to a phenomenon I call PDD (Post Deity Depression): "I've just met God," they say, "It should be the happiest day of my life; so why do I feel so crabby?" Don't worry. I'll explain.

The discerning among you may wish to know how I gathered together so much information on the After-Life. Would it surprise you to learn that the information has ALWAYS been there?! I am no scholar. I am no great or original thinker.

All I have done is to use techniques I recently learned on an MBA course in data-processing to make available, in a reader-friendly format, the pooled knowledge of the dead. I am merely a stringer-together of other peoples' beads.

This is how it was done: With the help of the New Jersey Assembly of Spiritualists, Psychics and Mediums, whose Headquarters are at Toms River, I have interviewed 14,231 dead people, from all walks of death, each one with their own unique story to tell. I will quote extensively from some of them at times, to illustrate and clarify aspects of the After-Life. Most of the people interviewed are just your average Joes and Joannas, but I was fortunate enough to tune into four people who were and still are famous: Pontius Pilate, James Joyce, Marlene Dietrich and Richard Nixon.

All interviews were taped on sophisticated, interactive EVPs that don't just record the voices of the dead, but now allow a two-way dialogue with the decarnate. So revolutionary is the technology that goes into these EVPs that I spent the last six months of this project hiding in cellars from the prying, satanic eyes of the CIA.

Having mentioned that arch-enemy of enlightenment, may I say here and now, with the certainty of the pure at heart that, as soon as this work is published, there will be a concerted campaign by the CIA and others to denigrate my findings. They don't want you to know. They want to keep you in ignorance, to maximize the sales of beads, cassocks, kaftans, chalices, Levi jeans, miters, kosher meat, and stained glass windows.

No doubt you have heard of William Whipple; he fell off his horse and broke his neck in 1785, but not before signing the Declaration of Independence: he it was who told me ten days ago that Thomas Jefferson is "mad as hell" that there is still no wall between the Government and God. "Despite our best intentions," thundered Jefferson from Beyond, "The Church and State have never been separate; they have always lived in sin; for there's no business like soul business."

This book, in its own small way, will complete what Jefferson started: put an end to the fear and uncertainty about the Great Beyond that governments for centuries have played on and abused. What this book says is 'basta!' No more lies! No more deceit! The Garden of Eden is not a piece of Real Estate for the privileged few; it was, is, and always will be a National Park.

America! The time has come to own your soul. It's been rented out for far too long to Christians, Muslims, Hindus, Buddhists, Jews, and those in charge of the Academy Awards. God has been shamefully misrepresented for more than 10,000 years. It's about time someone let Him do his own talking.

Who am I, you may ask: A passionate, old-fashioned crusader. I kiss, caress and ravish the Truth until we're both exhausted. I know, and do not care a fig for, the dangers of exposing myself like this, for the very first time, in public. I know in advance how much the findings of my work will be vilified and mocked (as all new spiritual insights are). The CIA may well track down my equipment and destroy it.

With this in mind, in the hope that the simple message of this book will not perish with me, I made a limited number of copies of my tapes of the dead, which are available to you, my dear friend, free of charge: proof, if proof were needed, that there will be no profit for this prophet. To order your copy, and to hear for yourself how clearly the dead can now speak, just phone 1-800 TALKINGDEAD; allow 3 months for delivery. They won't be available for long and, when they are gone, they are gone.

This, then, is the deal: by a combination of advanced technology, bloody-mindedness, and an ingenious questionnaire that I asked the departed to answer, I have been able to draw from the dead the most comprehensive spiritual and geographic map of Heaven that has ever been compiled. The Undiscovered country lies at last open and endless before you, as this great nation of ours once lay waiting to welcome those rugged pioneers.

So, now you are ready to embark on what will surely be the most astonishing read of your life. Keep this book by your bed at all times: when that private bank called The Federal Reserve calls in our loans, when Mother Earth finally works out how to choke us to death before we choke her, Heaven will be all that's left. As my dear old grandfather used to say, "Expect to die soon, and don't get caught with your spiritual pants down."

If you want to meet me in person, please go to The Blinding Light Bookshop, Camden, New Jersey, where I will spend most of my remaining days signing copies of this substantial work. Come soon, for the good die young, and I am fifty two.

God Bless!
J. F.

Chapter One

ARE YOU REALLY DEAD?

You've had these feelings all day; strange feelings; change feelings; transformations. Everything seems different somehow. The real is unreal and vice-versa. You've suddenly taken to floating. Not only do people look through you, you feel you can look through yourself. Nobody seems to notice you anymore; nobody cares about you; they'd walk all over you, if you didn't step out of their way.

Above your favorite diner a bright tunnel has appeared in the darkening sky. You are drawn to the tunnel, more than to the eggplant parmigiana, and endless cups of triple-caffeinated coffee available inside.

Indeed, for the first time in your life, you have no desire for eggplant parmigiana, no craving for caffeine. How can this be? Why are you suddenly the rope in this mysterious tug of war between the material and spiritual, the carnal comfort of the diner and the untextured mystery of the light? Surely this is not normal? Then it hits you: you're dead; you've passed over; you are being subsumed into the infinite. The awfully big adventure is at last about to begin.

Or is it? Are you really dead or are you just using this as an excuse not to go to work on Monday? Would it surprise you to learn that in my survey of the dead, 12.4% initially thought they were dead when they weren't. I should also say that a massive 42% who were well and truly dead went into denial and tried to swim against the tunnel's tide, which is ultimately useless and can cause severe spiritual strain.

In order, therefore, for you to have a well-adjusted passing-over and a self-confident apotheosis, I have drawn up a short list of infallible guidelines by which you can discover if you have ceased to be and, once you are sure you have, then the fun-fer-all, as James Joyce puts it, can begin.

It's not as easy as you may think to realize when you have passed over. You can have all the signs of death and not be dead at all.

Let me give you a few examples off the top of my head: are you registering no discernible brain activity? Well, maybe you are an Administrative Assistant in the local Vehicle Licensing Center.

Do you feel yourself to be a glowing, radiant being looking down from high on the tiny mortals below you? So do lawyers, every minute of their lives. Perhaps you find yourself shut up in a small box, never moving a muscle. It's ok, you are a worker in a toll-booth on the New Jersey Turnpike.

Do you see what I'm getting at? You need proof that you have died. You're not the one they give the certificate to. There's no paperwork up there. So study the following table before we press on.

Table 1.1

POSSIBLE SIGNS OF DEATH

SYMPTOMS	OTHER POSSIBLE CAUSES
Feeling of invisibility	Low self-esteem
Lack of interest in sex	Low self-esteem
Loss of appetite	Low self-esteem
People stop talking to you	Low self-esteem
Nobody hears what you say	Low self-esteem
You can't touch yourself anymore	Recent convert to Catholicism
You see people you thought were long dead	Rolling Stones' comeback concert
Your body doesn't seem to be yours anymore	Low self-esteem/ pregnant

All of the above MAY be signs that you have passed over, but NONE of them in themselves should be taken as gospel. Dying is a complicated business.

Once the spirit has been attached to the body, detachment is never smooth or simple.

It's not like peeling an orange; the spirit has permeated through the body and needs to be percolated carefully before it wafts away down the tunnel that connects the living to the dead.

In fact, the latest evidence suggests that the spirit rises up from the core of the body at death, splits up somewhere near the duodenum and works its way outwards in dozens of precious spiritual puffs which reunite to form the soul outside. Thus, bits of your spirit escape through the nose, bits through your mouth, bits through your pores and a sizeable portion enters the air outside via your rectum. Listen to the testimony of Christabel Atkins, who died in 1916:

> "It took three days for my soul to completely form after I choked to death eating ravioli. That part of my spirit which tried to emerge via the mouth was blocked inside the trachea until my throat was cut open by the doctor performing the autopsy. It was a weird feeling of spiritual incompleteness, not frightening, just odd, like my wedding night."

And Count Henri Simoniac, who died during the French Revolution:

> "Since my head was cut off, the whole of my spirit shot out—whoosh!—through my neck as fast as the fountain of blood. My soul was thus re-formed in four to five seconds. This is the big advantage of a violent death: spiritual exhilaration."

It's this variation in the time it takes for the soul to re-form that causes the most confusion initially in deciding whether you are dead or not. And some of the symptoms – detachment, confusion, loss of identity, frustration, endless waiting – are normal experiences in everyday life. A good place to study our second table, don't you think?

Table 1.2

PROBABLE SIGNS OF DEATH

SYMPTOM	Detachment
CAUSE, IF YOU ARE DEAD	Soul has re-formed outside the body and you are ready to leave this earth.
OTHER POSSIBLE CAUSES	Normal reaction after completing ten years as a high-school teacher and realizing you won't get a pension for another twenty.

SYMPTOM	Waiting in a Spiritual Limbo between this world and the next
CAUSE, IF YOU ARE DEAD	You're on your way to the Tunnel—it won't be long!
OTHER POSSIBLE CAUSES	You're an immigrant, waiting for a work permit, or you called a plumber a week ago.

SYMPTOM	**A delicious, floating sensation**
CAUSE, IF YOU ARE DEAD	You're testing your wings.
OTHER POSSIBLE CAUSES	Marijuana, or worse.

SYMPTOM	**Your body is on the bed, and you are high above**
CAUSE, IF YOU ARE DEAD	Farewell forever to flesh.
OTHER POSSIBLE CAUSES	Mirror on the ceiling, but you've yet to find someone as kinky as you are.

However, for you to be well and truly dead, for you to be certain that you'll never hear your heart beat again, never hold anyone's hand in yours, never make love, never eat, never sip Guinness, tea or whisky, never run, walk, drive, sleep, wake, dream, blink, stare, pee, crap, dress, undress, comb your hair or stroke your cat, three things have to happen.

1. Your spirit has to form completely outside your body;
2. You must see a tunnel open in the sky;
3. You must complete your journey through it.

Once you've crossed that border, the tunnel doesn't completely close, but instead of a highway to Heaven, it becomes a sort of ear-trumpet to the Earth, for those spirits so inclined to yell down and hope that someone hears them.

When you're dead, you can visit the tunnel and yell down it any time you wish but, for most souls, the novelty soon wears off and they find more interesting ways of spending eternity.

To sum up, if you ever strongly suspect you are dead, but aren't 100% sure, memorize this final table on the following page. This will give you the certainty you need to go forward. If you can say "yes" to each statement, you're dead, my friend, and life is about to begin!

Table 1.3

CERTAIN SIGNS OF DEATH

SYMPTOMS	OTHER POSSIBLE CAUSES
1. Complete re-formation of an everlasting soul, independent of the body.	None
2. Entrance into a Tunnel of spiritual light through which you are drawn at speed.	None
3. Emergence from the Tunnel, where preliminary arrangements are made for meeting God.	None

I will conclude this chapter with a brief description of the Tunnel Experience itself. If you learn nothing else, please learn this lesson: YOU MUST NOT IN ANY SHAPE OR FORM TRY TO RESIST THE TUG OF GOD.

The tunnel is your spiritual birth-canal and, once you have died, you cannot help being re-born into eternity, anymore than a baby can wiggle back into the womb, once they have been contracted out.

Remember, dying was the hard bit. After death you are not punished anymore. The Tunnel is meant to be a joyous Water-Slide, a streamlined, funfair connection between this world and the next. It is the first stage in an inconceivably vast and intricate magnetic coil, at the center of which is God. God is your mid-wife. Once you feel His tug, let yourself go with joy. If you do resist, the following problems may occur:

Spiritual distension

This is by far the most common ailment of the reluctant newly dead. Your spirit, at death, is a perfect copy of you and, though it must undergo certain transformations before the meeting with God, it is important that it remains as true to you as possible while you travel through the tunnel.

If you pull against the life-force, you will become unnecessarily extended and this stretching will hamper later efforts to achieve your Optimum Soul-Form. Spiritual damage incurred while traveling through the tunnel is much harder to repair than other damage sustained in your mortal life. Pontius Pilate had a particularly bad trip:

> "I was worried about dying more than most, for reasons I'd rather not go into. When my time came, therefore, and the tunnel appeared, I turned around and made strong swimming motions, which I believe you now call the breaststroke. I was a good swimmer, but it didn't help.

> "I tried to hang onto the sides of the Tunnel, but it hasn't got any. Instead of moving back to Earth, though, all that happened was that my legs kept getting stretched towards the light.

"Finally, of course, I became exhausted and was pulled the wrong way into Eternity, which is a bad beginning. I could hardly stand when I emerged on the other side: when I was alive, I was five foot three and fat; after my resistance to the tunnel, I stood twenty-four foot two inches tall and had a three inch waist. God has been good, though, since then."

Optimum Soul Form, for those of you who don't know, is the spiritual reflection of how your body should have looked when you were twenty-four, if you had taken better care of it or, in some cases, if you had managed to make it that far.

As you journey down the magnetic coil, there are certain intricate repairs made to you to mould you into this shape – a sort of drive-through soul-enhancer – and how long you take to complete the process depends on the relative waywardness of your life.

The process can take anything from five minutes, in the case of St. Francis of Assisi, to fifteen thousand years, in the case of some very wicked cavemen. There is no Hell, by the way, in the eternal sense; the Jews were right, at least on this point, but I digress. (See Chapter 3.)

Soiling the Soul

You can't meet God until your spirit is pure light. The Tunnel is like a car-wash: it sprays you with a coating of light as you pass through. It is so set as to be at its most efficient if you travel through with your "arms" and "legs" extended and your soul completely relaxed.

If you wriggle and twist and squirm, you won't receive the full benefit of this sophisticated first step to transcendence. In short, you will come out covered in black spots. These spots will be removed later, but it can be a painful operation. Heed the words of Martha, from Minneapolis:

> "I was a wriggler, I was a resister, I came out of that tunnel so blotchy you wouldn't believe it. I cried when I saw how white and pure and good the others looked. I was so ashamed. I wondered why I couldn't be as lovely and white as they were. I mean white in the spiritual sense.
>
> "There ain't no black and white up here, but I can't tell you what I mean until you come and see for yourself. They took them blotches off later but, man, did it hurt. I tell you, you don't need that pain. You make sure you're good and relaxed when you die, or it won't be no picnic. Ok?"

Tailbacks and Tunnel-Rage

The Tunnel can get crowded. Think of earthquakes, think of famine, think of war, think of the billions of Big Macs that have been sold all over the world. Tailbacks in the tunnel are, unfortunately, an unavoidable fact of death.

You may find yourself in a humdinger. You may not move for several months or years. You must remain in control; you mustn't lose your rag: don't succumb to the rage that may well up in you if another soul cuts in front of you or won't allow you to merge into the mainstream. Here are some final handy hints to help you cope with potential frustration:

1. NEVER FORGET THAT YOU ARE DEAD: even if you are stuck in the tunnel for a thousand years, it really doesn't matter because you are now immortal. Time, in fact, has ceased to be, but this takes a while to sink in.

2. HUM SOFTLY TO YOURSELF: It doesn't have to be a hymn; in fact hymns are sung mainly by people on Earth. In the Next World, songs by the Beatles, Elvis Presley, Nick Drake and Leonard Cohen are more common when spirits have a get-together.

3. LEARN ANOTHER LANGUAGE: Take a look around; talk to the guy beside you. Try to become fluent in his language, if it's different from yours. If he's German, a thousand years will go by in a flash, and you still won't have mastered irregular verbs.

4. MORE HASTE, LESS SPEED: Remember, those who cut in front of you and push other souls out of the way will not get to where they are going any quicker: they will need lengthy spiritual repair work later in one of the thousands of soul-shops just outside the tunnel. Move gently and calmly through the tunnel, as though you were born in England.

Chapter Two

NOW THAT YOU ARE DEAD

HOW YOU MAY BE FEELING

The first thing that needs to be said, now that you have snuffed it is: Congratulations! You've joined the great majority. All the best people are dead and you, at last, are one of them. So, there you are, my friend: splendid and radiant on the other side of the tunnel, an individual beam of light, a fully recognizable Form, lacking genitals, and all the better for it.

The Earth is your home no more. Once you move towards the brilliant white, dome-shaped Astrum at present just a tiny dot in the distance, you will never see, or miss, the Earth again. My advice is: DON'T LOOK BACK! Most newly-deads, of course, do, and are universally amazed at the puniness and insignificance of what they used to feel such love for.

The first question most people want to have answered is who they will spend eternity with. Or, as Tom Morgan puts it more crudely, "It won't be the wife, will it?"

The answer is yes, and no. When one organ meets another, souls do not always commune. If there was love, though, your love will eventually be there. Giuseppe Pavone, from Pisa explains:

> "I was married, but loved another. When I came out of the tunnel, this woman was standing with her back to me. Slim, with long, dark, ethereal hair. I thought it might be my wife, and that I'd gone to Hell. She turned round and I wept for joy: it was Maria. I couldn't believe my luck; my wife had found out, and killed both of us."

So, there you have it: you will spend eternity with those whom you wish to spend it with; simple, straightforward, heavenly!

There are none of the tedious complications in relationships up there that we have to put up with down here: if you never want to see someone you knew on earth again, you never will.

Thus, some spirits spend eternity with their lover, some with their parents, some with friends, some with their spouse (or spouses), and some, if such be their essence and heart's desire, magnificently alone.

Animals, too, are given special dispensation to live on in spirit form, if the love-bond between them and their owner had been strong enough during their earthly existence. I have been moved to tears by the pure and heartfelt joy of souls who have been reunited with their cat, their dog, their budgie, their pony, their donkey and their goldfish.

What happens, though, if you get tired of a fellow spirit over there? What if you make a mistake? Is it eternal, this time? Hell, no! Such circumstances are rare, but when they do occur, because we have no ego, the unwanted party telepathically understands in an instant, and simply disappears – puff! – in gentle dissolution, with no hard feelings on their part, or wasteful guilt on yours.

The purity and sheer common sense of relationships on the other side is, in itself, worth dying for.

Before we close this section, more should be said about the problem of denial, touched on earlier. 42% of the dead felt their souls detach, saw the tunnel open, went down the tunnel and even emerged on the other side, still denying the evidence of their super senses. James Joyce readily admits to having been one of the worst offenders.

"My first reaction," he told me, "was 'I don't fucking believe this gob-shite.'"

The After-Life, it has to be said, comes as a shock to most atheists. Joyce was pleased, though, when God himself was reported to have started reading, and not been able to finish, *Finnegans Wake*. Joyce is now happily at work deconstructing the telepathic system of communication and making pure energy obscene.

Richard Nixon still won't admit that he is dead, as this recent taped interview with a soul counselor shows:

> "I am not a corpse; it is abhorrent to every bone in my body to quit the earth. Who are you to tell me I am dead? You're a Jew aren't you? Or queer. Or both. Bastard."

Someone who voted for Nixon, Stanley Markowitz, a construction worker from Philadelphia, explains the hard time he had coming to terms with "all this new spiritual crap" after he had a fatal heart attack while beating up a Dallas Cowboys fan at a football game:

> "One minute, ya know, I'm there, what's the word, eh, pummeling this low-life and the next, it's all lights and tunnels an' flying an all this love yer fuckin' neighbor type of shit. An' I'm 'yeah, right, this ain't happenin' – an' it is happenin' an' you ain't got no choice, you ain't got no control, you gotta be, you know, a stinkin' spirit from now on. They don't give you no fuckin' choice. It ain't American. It ain't democratic. Ok, so, how am I gonna spend eternity? Shit, I'm just fuckin' sittin' 'ere – I ain't goin' nowhere, no-how."

Interestingly, it is almost always men who deny that they are dead. Women, once they've died, tend to open themselves immediately to the new experiences, and adapt readily to the idea of a life of everlasting communication and oneness with the Absolute. Listen to Jane Carte, a feminist from Chelsea, England, who died in 1966:

> "One would have thought that here, of all places, issues of gender would finally be resolved. Not a bit of it, darling. Men are still into the power trip; some of them abuse and make fun of angels, few of them are in any hurry to meet God because, I suppose, God is not the authoritarian patriarch and fascist who, in their hearts, they used to worship. And they're so childish and directionless, without their penis to hold onto."

These brief testimonies should give you some indication that fore-warned is fore-armed. You can waste a lot of spiritual energy by being negative when you're dead. You still have will-power, the journey is what you make it, but there are certain self-evident truths about the Next World which, if you accept them now, while you're alive, will make your journey as pleasant as apple juice. These self-evident truths are:

1. Eternity is forever.
2. Even you are immortal
3. God wants a Word.

Bear these three facts constantly in mind, and you won't go too far wrong.

WHAT YOU MAY BE CONCERNED ABOUT

1. S-E-X.

Let us, once and for all, put to bed this hoary chestnut: I have asked every dead person I know if, and how, they get it on, and every dead person I know has said the same: there is no sex in the next world.

How could there be? You have no body and, therefore no bodily functions. There are advantages to this: the dead do not have sex, but nor do they have diarrhea.

You are, remember, destined to become a spirit: a small, pure pulse of self-sustaining light. Nothing goes into you anymore and, therefore, there is nowhere for it to come out. And, by nothing, I mean nothing. There is no sight, for you have no eyes; no sound, for you have no ears; no taste, for you have no tongue; no touch, for you have no hands; no smell, for you have no nose. Ultimately, there are no words and, if it weren't for the fact that you and I are still alive, I wouldn't be even writing like this, so far away words are from the apprehension I have gained of what is really real.

This is my difficulty: try to understand, when I say, without arrogance, that I am enlightened, and you are not. I know the futility of words in Heaven, but how else except in languid language can I explain my vision to you? Even Dante apologized for his poetry; with some justification, I may add.

Anyway, I don't want to get too technical. All I can say is this: put your body behind you, and think in terms of light. There is no sex in the bright Beyond, not even tantric – which (believe me, I know, having tried it) was a cheap West Coast commercial fabrication. There is love. What more do you want?

2. Do Dead Friends and Dead Relatives Witness our Intimate Moments On Earth?

Apparently, I'm afraid to say, some do. As I explain in more detail in the next chapter, once the novelty of being dead wears off, things can get a little boring as preparations are made to visit God in the Astral Dome.

There is a sense of peace and well-being, but the earth is still in range and can be, for some, an irresistible attraction. You don't actually visit the Earth as such, you project yourself there astrally. The psychic energy released by this projection enables you to experience the journey as though you were still alive, and influence material objects by sheer force of will.

Astral Travel is available to us all while we are alive, through the medium of sleep. In dreams, we are – or feel ourselves to be – present at events in the now, the was, or the will be.

I seem to be rooted in the past. So far, in dreams that I remember, I have been a Roman soldier, a Vietnam G.I., a groundling at the world premiere of Hamlet, an Egyptian princess, and an orange in Nell Gwynne's basket. I became these things – and hundreds more – as sleep dissolved the artificial barriers to time and space we all erect when conscious. The dead have a deeper understanding of this process, and some of them use it as entertainment, in the absence of cable TV.

So, dear Reader, be warned: if you are on your own, doing you know what, and the box of tissues you thought you placed beside you suddenly isn't there, it might not be your forgetfulness; it might well be your mother, or worse. Similarly, when you are straining on the toilet, grateful that no-one can see you, for your dignity would be so impaired, and the Michael Jackson song 'You Are Not Alone' comes wafting in through the window, that is not, I'm afraid, a coincidence.

You are not alone
I am here with you
Though I may be far...

Don't be too hard on the dead. They're not Peeping Toms. They are just passing what used to be time.

3.   Is There Baseball in The After-Life?
No.

4.   What Sports Do The Departed Play, Then?
Soccer. Just soccer.

5.   I'm an Atheist, So Why am I in Heaven?
Good question, and one that many ask themselves the moment they see the tunnel. Consider this, you recalcitrant non-believers: according to a recent survey, the people most likely to have studied the Bible in depth are atheists.

Card-carrying Christians figure prominently among the band of devout believers who have never given the Good Book so much as a backward glance. Atheists study the Bible in order to prove it wrong; Christians don't need to study the Bible, because they know it is right.

It therefore becomes a win-win situation for the so-called Christian God, in that the Bible becomes important for both parties. It is important for the first party, because they need to know what it says in order to reject it; it is important to the second party as a symbol of what they stand for, like a tattoo.

I had a reconciled atheist explain this to me from beyond the grave: you can't be an atheist unless you think about God; God doesn't ask for much: all He wants you to do is think about Him occasionally.

Since atheists meet this criterion, they go, will-they nil-they, with the rest of us, through the tunnel. The other important criterion, of course, is that, whether we like it or not, we all have immortal souls.

6. Whatever Happened to Hell?

I wasn't at all happy when all my sources confirmed that the wicked are not punished. I'm an average Joe. I'd like to see murderers rot in Hell as much as the next guy. It's not my fault that they don't, nor, perhaps is it my job to speculate as to why God has seen fit not to punish evil bastards.

Anyway, he hasn't. We all travel the same path after death; some of us need more work than others to scrape away impurities and warts, but no one suffers in eternal fire, or I would certainly have heard them.

Perhaps we are not yet mature enough to cope with the idea that there is minimal reward for being good, but the fact remains that the afterlife is as much a process as this one. It's just that we don't worship processes as much as we should, precisely because they are "common."

Think of the wonders of our digestive system: miracles occur daily in the entrails of us all, but morality plays little part in these transformations. The food that went down Hitler's throat did not come back up protesting.

What more is there to say? There is no Hell. We'll all be happy when we die. Get used to it.

7. The Weight of the Soul

Where, though, does the energy come from to transform us into a beam of light after we die? The answer comes from a judicious fusion of psychic investigation and quantum physics.

The soul has mass whilst in the body, and this mass is converted, by spiritual self-fission, into eternal energy. It was established long ago, by the great William Mac-Dougall of Oxford University, that the soul weighs 21 grams.

With astonishing persistence and dedication to the betterment of us all, he went round houses and hospitals looking for those on the point of death, and weighed them just before they died, and immediately after.

After attending hundreds of death bed scenes the length and breadth of England with his trusty scales, he announced, to a sadly indifferent world, that he had proven the existence of the soul.

He was the first to discover that all humans, whether a 400-pound sumo wrestler or a newborn baby, lose 21 grams the moment they became a corpse. As is to be expected of an Oxford man, he was a meticulous and conscientious scientist: if any matter of any kind left the corpse through any orifice, he made sure that it was included in his calculations as the weight of the body after death.

This attention to detail made the findings of his work irrefutable: there was no observable loss of matter before and after death, so where had the 21 grams gone to? There could, he quite rightly claimed, be no other explanation than a spiritual one.

The weight represented the soul, taking up space in the body, and therefore contributing to the body's weight in that mysterious fusion of the divine and the animal that is our undeniable essence.

This weight – 21 grams – is precisely the amount of matter required, as any modern day quantum physicist will tell you, to convert us into the beam of pure light we become when we re-form outside the body and shoot towards the Tunnel.

This fact must also be of some comfort to the growing legions of the obese in America: there is no obesity in the next world: we will all weigh 21 grams for a few moments, and then nothing at all forever.

PREVIOUS AFTERLIFE GUIDEBOOKS

Why were previous guide books to the next world so wrong? Why are the earliest descriptions of where we go to when we die so uniformly depressing?

Eat my dust, Gilgamesh; fight a serpent, Pharaoh; pay the ferryman, Greeko, and let him paddle you to Shitland, Firetown, Dustville and Wormwoods. Don't even get me started on Dante. God, it makes me so mad, they told such lies.

Imagine how pissed you'd be if you were a Pharaoh, and spent your whole life learning spells from The Book of The Dead, so you could sail towards the Northern Gate, past the fields of turquoise, stopping off to weigh a few peasants' hearts against a feather, before you open the door of the Mansion of He Who Finds Faces, and become one with the sun, for the benefit of all, only to die and find out it's all bollocks.

I did actually get through to a Pharaoh and, he was so embarrassed at being duped by his priests, he refused to give me his name. He did say he died young and had spent all of his young life, and the equivalent of $457,232,650 preparing for tests of endurance, as written down in The Book of The Dead, which never actually happened.

All that he experienced was what we all experience: what I am setting out here before you so simply, in this book. I told him that modern Americans can learn the secrets of death from me – for a measly seven bucks – and boy, was he pissed.

Why were they so wrong? Simple. They were wrong because they had no science then, no technology, and some of them were just bare-faced liars.

So, thank your lucky stars you live in the 21st century, with EVPs and ghost detectors scientifically monitoring the dead, and putting paid to such crass superstition, by capturing the next world on video and audio tape.

Science and common-sense has prevailed and triumphed in our time to such an extent that all subsequent generations will have to do is thank us.

I myself feel privileged to have been born in the right place, at the right time, and thus to be the first to bring you this Good News. I am humbled by the awesomeness of my mission, and cannot, in truth, comprehend the sheer magnitude of what I am doing.

But, this isn't about me: it's about you.

And the Good News I bring is: you don't have to read much anymore to know eternal truths; in fact, all you need to do is read this book.

In case you were thinking of reading what I call the Deathly Classics, under the delusion of possible enlightenment, let me make it clear: you would simply be wasting your time.

All previous books on the afterlife are nothing but dangerous disinformation; I myself have read these books in a spirit of altruism, so you don't have to.

So I say to all of you who want to prepare for eternity as practically as you can, and who have such busy lives: don't read Gilgamesh; don't read The Book of The Dead; don't read about Odysseus in The Underworld; don't read The Bible, The Koran, The Bodhisattva, or whatever it is that Hindus read. And for God's sake, don't read bloody Dante – he gets it right occasionally but damn, is he anal-retentive!

Before we end this section, I must say a word about the trustworthiness of the Dead. It has been assumed by many cultures that what the Dead say is always true. I can tell you now: no, it isn't. The Dead have a mischievous sense of humor, and can communicate idiocies to deceive us all.

Witness the New Age section of so many independent bookstores. New Agers in particular seem to have been fed more false information than most by the Dead, but they generally take this in good heart when they pass over.

Perhaps my favorite dead Hippie is Simon Shakkarak. Simon died in San Francisco in 2012 and attended Woodstock in 1969, where he was the victim of Henry Haight, a nineteenth-century banker who doesn't like what Hippies have done to that part of San Francisco which is named after him:

> "Man, what a trip my death was! From the haze and the highs and the hugs of Haight-Ashbury to meeting the real Henry Haight in spirit form! Henry Haight is something else. When any Hippie dies, Henry is first to greet them, on the Other Side, waving a banner that says *Let's Roast Another Hippie.*
>
> "Hey, it's cool man. Turns out Henry was the guy who freaked me out at Woodstock by taking over my Ouija board, and leaving messages we wrote books about years later. *There's bad acid in the dahl, dude; George Carlin's gonna get ya; where you're not is where it's at.* A freaking dead banker messing with our heads at Woodstock! Man, that's messed up!"

How, you may legitimately ask at this point, do I myself know that the dead are not doing the same to me?

How can I be sure that I am not deluded? How have I ensured objectivity and truth?

Simple: I am a scientist first, and an artist in my spare time. My background in data-processing, and my expertise in testing techniques have proven invaluable in the verification of what I am told.

The sheer volume of interviews I have made, the complicated cross-questioning, the endless hours I have spent devising tests to ensure the dead don't trick me, the cross-cultural diversity of my samples ensure the success of my venture.

The scientists among you are welcome to audit all of this any time you like, for a small fee. This part of my project has, I admit, been the most time-consuming and tedious, but has proven to be immensely worthwhile.

I will not bore you, the general reader, with science and statistics. I will just say what should be a mantra for our times: trust me, I'm a scientist.

Chapter Three

BE PREPARED

*T*he soul is a wonderful thing. It is indestructible. Just think about that, for a moment.

Whatever you do to a soul, it can never be destroyed. They can take you into a desert, chain you to the ground, bring out the most powerful nuclear bomb in existence, position it over you, and drop it on you personally, so that it explodes an inch from your eyeball. Your body is vaporized, your atoms are atomized, there isn't so much as a quark left to show you once existed.

And what does your soul say to all this?

'Is that all you've got, pal?! You just wasted $50,000,000, and not so much as a dent in me to show for it.'

And, with every newborn baby, another one of these indestructible wonders is brought into the world. I want you to think about that. Humbly, but with awe.

We may now continue our journey.

When I started this project seven years ago, as a rookie monitor of the decarnate, armed only with a bottom of the range EVP recorder that I bought on eBay, the first question I invariably asked the departed was: "How long have you been dead?"

How they laughed at my ignorance! How raw and hopelessly life-centered my question must have seemed to those who are, of course, beyond time's dull deceptions!

An unpublished dead poet called Carly, who wrote without success in San Francisco from 1958-1972, put it this way:

> "The living are death's virgins; time is life's hymen: it falls with you, withered, or ruptured into the grave. You are not, as you so quaintly put it on your side, 'a long time dead'. You are *no time dead*. There is no time in death. There is no death in time. Think about it, you flesh-soiled son-of-a-bitch, and stop asking me such stupid fucking questions!"

I'm sorry to say that I have had problems with all the dead poets I have reached. Anger, bitterness, betrayal, scorn, disappointment and paranoia are what I have come to expect from those who, before they passed, put down their thoughts in verse. There seems to be some sort of residual resentment that sets in among these creative types. Perhaps it's different with successful poets, but I have not yet contacted a dead and published poet which, statistically, is not surprising.

Not being a poet myself, I can't quite grasp where they're coming from, or going to. I sensed that Carly, though dead, had anger-management issues, and still had not overcome the temporal disappointment of having her soul-work rejected by every publishing company in America; including, sadly, one her own father ran.

On a more cheerful note, hundreds of other, more practical decarnates gave me similar information about time, in a much simpler and clearer manner, which I will summarize thus: Time, as we know it, dies when we do. It is replaced by a state of *no-time*.

You cannot hope to understand no-time while the concept 'Be there at 8am sharp' still makes sense to you. Those of you who are, in life, incurably tardy, and invariably late for anything where a time is mentioned may be cheered to know that you are preparing for eternity, which is the death of time, in a much more practical manner than I myself, a 'tight-assed, punctual, clock-driven passive-aggressive,' as I was once described by a friend.

Indeed, the only thing I, personally, need to work on before I die is how to miss appointments. I am better prepared than anyone in history for my own death, except in this one niggling deficiency: I can't help looking at the clock. I know there will be no clocks in Heaven; I know that time will dissolve and yet, every single night before I go to sleep, aware as I am of eternity, I set and test the alarm.

What can I say? I'm human.

Adjusting to no-time is just the first step. All the dead must see God. That's a law, which I'll explain soon. But God is nothing if not busy: moving the sun and other stars, presiding over the explosions of super-nova, creating thousands of new life forms every second takes up a lot of His valuable no-time.

How is He going to fit in a personal interview with each and every one of us, even if that interview consists of just one word?

The answer is simple enough: as God has to see billions of humans, and trillions of what we at present call aliens, as well as supervise the efficient functioning of the Universe and its parallels, He can only see us in the next world on what we used to call Tuesdays.

This means that, when you emerge from the tunnel, you have to wait your turn. If you prepare for this indefinite waiting period now, while still alive, it will make the choices offered to you when you are dead all the more simple.

I describe the specific activities available to you during this waiting period in the next chapter, but it would do no harm at all, while you are alive, to consider in particular whether, when you are dead, you would like to revisit people on earth, which is a popular pastime during this stage of the afterlife; if you intend to come back from the grave, here's some practical advice.

While you are still alive, make a short list of those you would like to contact when you die. If they are open to the idea, ask their permission to visit them when you are dead, and explain how you will visit them (Astral Projection, as an orb, on a Ouija board, subliminal messages on their favorite cable TV program, etc).

Some people don't like being visited by the dead, and it is best to find this out while they are alive: it could ruin things for your relationship after you both die if you scare the hell out of him by making your picture fall off the wall, turning her tap on in the bathroom, or leaving a message from the next world on his iPad.

It is, though, a sound and sensible idea to get a head start on death, and develop the spiritual gifts you will be using in the next world while you are still in this one. This will help you not only to haunt people, but also to understand the state of being dead before it happens.

There are many ways you can practice being dead. First of all, by vibrating.

As you may know, we all vibrate at different frequencies, the higher the frequency, the more advanced the state of being, from the slow, stately waltz of atheists, to the frenetic rock and roll of psychics. God, of course vibrates at every modular frequency imaginable, so you can always never quite tune in to him.

The more you practice vibrating at different frequencies while alive, the smoother your transition will be to the spirit world.

When you try the following exercises, though, it's important not to vibrate too much – you don't want to lose consciousness, or prematurely transform yourself into a higher being such as a Hathon.

Follow these directions step by step, and you'll be fine. First, choose a peaceful room with limited light, and lie down on the floor.

Close your eyes, and wiggle your toes. Start off slowly, with the big toe, keeping the others perfectly still. Then, wiggle each individual toe in turn, without moving any other. Once you have mastered this, create your own cosmic toe dance, moving slow and fast, two at a time, six at a time, all of them together, and so on.

Consciously imitate the rhythm of known dances and feel the vibrations caress the soles of your feet, energize your legs and use this energy to expand in corporal and spiritual bliss. The pleasure is indescribable!

What is actually happening is that the vibration is transmitted to the memory of every single cell in your body, and billions of separate cellular consciousnesses interconnect to replicate, as it were, an elemental music.

You are starting to transcend the limpid state of three dimensions, and your naturally interdimensional DNA leaps and twists in joy as it is released from the humdrum and unfulfilling task of merely maintaining life, to delight in pure spirituality. You cannot, in fact, hope to live a life of the spirit until you understand that the universe itself is a vibrator.

The second way you can practice being dead is by listening to lots of music. Not passively, but transcendentally. Music suspends time.

Music is the simplest way to enter into a state of no-time that the living have. Music keeps you young.

I am a living example of this. I'm 52 years old, but my face is 23. This was not achieved by diet or exercise, but by lying on the couch for hours on end listening to

Mozart, Black Sabbath, Judy Collins, The Grateful Dead, Hannah Montana, Nick Drake, Verdi, Irish and Iranian Folk music, Leonard Cohen, The Sex Pistols, and Ray Charles.

The diversity is all important: the infinite variety of vibrations to which my being was exposed kept it in a god-like, timeless state of suspended animation, so that four hours of listening to Ozzy Osbourne literally took four weeks off my face.

The important thing is not to listen to the words, or the story, or the chords, or anything that the musicians themselves claim to be important. Bathe in music, like milk. Let it sweep over you without reflecting on it in any way. You will then experience the phenomenon of no-time, and will be closer to death, in a positive way, than the silkiest of Shamans.

I should mention here the most beautiful of music known to a man: that of a woman's voice. We men are blessed that women feel compelled to talk so much, because the sweet vibration of their voice-box is divinely designed to reproduce the harmony of the next world.

Whatever your gender, or sexual proclivity, when you listen to a woman talking, treat it as you would treat music: bathe in the form, though the actual content at times may wash over you. This is, though women don't yet know it, the ultimate act of love from a man.

A man in love with a woman is so entranced by the music of her voice, that he doesn't always have the capacity to decipher the actual words. He enters into this blissful state of no-time, only to be rudely awoken at times by the cold coda: 'why don't you friggin listen?'

This is harsh. We *do* listen. We listen so well that we are transported beyond the now, to the timeless. When we focus on the content, we lose the form. So, despite current popular prejudice to the contrary, the more a man actually listens to a woman, the less he loves her.

I'd better move on. We've talked about what to do, now on to what not to do. The worst way you can prepare for the next world is, as I touched on above, by being religious. By this, I mean feeling the need to join, or renew membership of, a religious institution.

I was a Catholic. I went to mass 1,321 times. A lifelong Catholic may go to more than 5,000. A priest may go to his grave having said mass 40,000 times or more. And they never change the script. Not a single word, not a single gesture.

Hey, let's be honest: how many times can you see your favorite movie before you start to hate it? And, I'm talking Hollywood – multi-million dollar budgets, special effects, the best actors and scripts in the world. However decent my local priest was, his budget was the collection plate, and he'd clearly never been to voice school. The whole show was monotone, and the only special effect – a damn good one, called transubstantiation – you had to imagine for yourself.

I would like to conclude this chapter by bringing it into the now. A few seconds ago – as I typed the word 'transubstantiation' – my computer screen went wonky. I did what I always do in such circumstances – banged the screen hard and pressed keys F1-F12 rapidly at random. Words appeared shakily on the screen. I tried to make them out, but could not. My heart began to pound. I felt this might be a message from the dead priest of my formative years, whose spirit I had just evoked. I did not, though, feel the psychic thrill that genuine messages from the dead invariably give me. My skeptical instincts – developed over 30 years – proved correct.

When the words finally formed, it was not a message from the next world; it was a message from the Norton Company, which protects my computer. "An attack on your computer has just been detected," it read.

"Yes, you idiot," I shouted back in exasperation, "it was me."

I include this anecdote purely to re-enforce the message that I am not deluded; everything recorded in this book is there because it actually happened, and its authenticity is fully documented.

Any apparent contact with the next world which contained the tiniest possibility of not being paranormal has been rigorously omitted. Only when the keys of my computer moved themselves did I save the message to my *Psychic* folder.

Messages on my Ouija board were only deemed acceptable when I and my assistant, Diana, were blindfolded and the whole process videoed by cameras I have all over my bedroom. One-way dialogue captured on my EVPs was only stamped 'authentic' after ten separate people – including a high school drop-out, an atheist and a non-American confirmed they had heard the exact same form of words.

My numerous two-way conversations with the dead have all been confirmed as 'beyond doubt from beyond the grave,' by the New Jersey Assembly of Spiritualists, Psychics, and Mediums, whose approbation is a guarantee of paranormal gold.

I am talking about things I have sensed and voices I have heard and souls I have talked to and recorded. All is scientific. All is objective. All is true.

Let us advance to the Plane of the Waiting Dead, and reveal its dark mysteries.

Chapter Four

THE EARLY DAYS OF INFINITY

*N*ot much happens at first, once you become a beam of pure light. There's a lot of waiting around. Many people imagine that once you have been released from your body, you can go anywhere you like in the universe, and spend eternity on an endless, free vacation.

Well, you can't.

First of all, you are not in the universe – you're dead. You are on an entirely different plane. Where you are – commonly called *The Indeterminate Plane* – is a waiting room. A very beautiful landscape of circles, curves and inter-connected light, but a waiting room nonetheless.

There are three main circles. The first is dedicated to Education and Self-Betterment, and is thronged by the Wise and the Eager to Learn.

The second circle, commonly called 'Souls Reunited' is a very useful meeting place where you are given a list of everyone you knew who is now dead, and invited to add them as friends, in which case, they will manifest themselves to you telepathically, or discretely ignore them, in which case, they won't.

You are also given the option of meeting six famous dead people for possible long-term relationships, depending on how compatible you prove. This service is, I am told, the most disappointing: if there was someone in history who was your absolute Hero, I would advise you to keep them alive in your imagination alone. Various souls have told me how sorry they ultimately were to meet Robin Hood, Karl Marx, Billy the Kid, Houdini, Abraham Lincoln, Moses, Shakespeare and Jezebel. None of them, it seems, lived up to expectations. An anonymous Russian Professor left a message on my EVP just before we went to press, saying he'd just met Tolstoy, and calling him something less than a Count.

The Third Circle is a window onto the world of dead aliens, who make up over 98% of the soul community. They have their own path, and their own passage, and there is no actual communing with them, but you can admire their wondrous forms and shapes through millions of devices that act like telescopes into these parallel eternities.

If you've ever watched *Star Trek*, *Star Wars*, or *Dr Who*, you may be gratified to know that none of the aliens from those series are, strictly speaking, fictional: they were all planted in their creators' minds by Astral Projection.

Klingons, Cybermen, Vogons, Jedi, Kodos, Kungas, Parnithacs, Kleptumbalii, Lithuanians and Darth Veda all exist. There is, in fact, no such thing as fiction: every character ever imagined in any book, however worthless, is a reflection of an actual existing entity that the 'author' has psychically picked up. Even Daleks have souls, and you can watch them drift, bewildered, to their particular destination from several vantage points, as you wait to meet your God.

The waiting is well managed. You are informed, very early on, telepathically, by Angels, that while preparations are being made for you to visit God in the Astral Dome, which is, at the moment, merely a dot in the distance, you are free to explore the Indeterminate Zone-from top to bottom circle, or visit the Earth through Astral Projection.

For those who need help with their astral projection technique, there are courses on hand from former Spiritualists and Zen Masters. In fact, the whole first circle of the Indeterminate Zone is packed with opportunities for self-betterment and relaxation. It is popularly known as *The Mansion*.

There are many rooms in *The Mansion,* all of them fully equipped with everything you need to become perfect, or perfectly content. You can learn a new afterlife skill, listen to the greatest singers and entertainers since time began, or finally get round to writing that novel you never found time for while alive. Best of all, there's no charge. No charge whatsoever.

It's hard, at first, to get used to the concept that there are no fees whatsoever for Education in the Afterlife. We are so used to paying for everything down here, especially in America, that then we die and discover that there is no monetary system anymore, it requires quite an adjustment.

Since life on Earth is a preparation for the Afterlife, the puzzling fact we all have to confront is that, for all the material gifts it has given us, spiritually, Capitalism is a dead end.

Geoff, a hard working Merchant Banker from New York, explains how he had to change his entire value system when he died:

> "I wanted to do an advanced course in Astral Projection, in order to guide my wife through the intricacies of selling our apartment below. She's much younger, and more naïve than me, and I was worried that, without me, she'd get ripped off.
>
> "I was told you could communicate with the living through Astral Projection, and I wanted to plant this message in my wife's mind while she was dreaming: 'Don't take less than $4,000,000, and watch those bastards when they try to sneak in closing costs.'
>
> "I enrolled in the class of Paramhansa Yogananda, famous on Earth for manifesting himself in ectoplasm, and in Heaven for the informality of his open air lectures. I asked him how much it would cost to transfer knowledge from his mind to mine. He said 'Give me everything that's in your pockets.'
>
> "I didn't have any pockets, and was puzzled. Apparently it was a joke. A joke that was part of my training. I didn't realize this until much later. He then asked me to go search Heaven, and find Wall Street.
>
> "I searched *The Indeterminate Plane* for the equivalent of five years: Wall Street isn't actually here. Finally, I got the message, 'revelation,' as they call it: none of the qualities

of financial expertise that helped me thrive on Earth are of any use whatsoever up here, because everything here is free. That's one hell of a shock when you've known nothing else when alive but Merchant Banking.

"I'm adapting, sure, but I'm still a little pissed that, by the time I mastered Astral Projection, and sent the message, my wife had left the Earth to join me and had, of course long ago been taken to the cleaners by Goldman Sachs."

The teachings of Paramhansa Yogananda, though, bore fruit, and the last time I spoke to Geoff, he had just heard that God could see him now, and has begun the journey I will take you on in the next chapter.

Before we go there, a word about the fantastic entertainment on offer in the Indeterminate Zone, which may make some of you hope to die tomorrow. Thousands of the dead whom I have interviewed place this as the best way to pass the time while you wait to meet God.

All have spoken breathlessly about the wonders they have seen here. Entertainers and Artists get the option of staying in the Indeterminate Zone indefinitely, if they agree to perform for the masses.

This has made 'Sweet Chariots' by far the most popular club in Heaven, and no wonder: Homer sings *The Odyssey* and *Iliad* each night, while Frank Sinatra croons next door; Roman Acrobats, Greek Thesbians and Babylonian Flute players cavort and entertain the throngs who pack the sidewalks waiting to get in.

Ten thousand year old songs from China, India and Mongolia hang delicately before you in fragrant bouquets of bliss; T.S. Eliot recites *The Love Song of Alfred J Prufrock,* endlessly, outside 'The Poet's Club.'

Inside the club you will find real poets: Walt Whitman, Pablo Neruda, Baudelaire, Pushkin, W.B. Yeats, Chaucer, John Donne, Chu' Yuan, Tu-Fu (the 'Chinese Keats' – Keats himself is still too shy to perform), Mohammed Iqbal, Goethe, Petrarch, Pavese, Virgil, Catullus, Horace, Pindar, Sappho, Per Atterbom (a gifted genius, who made poetry out of Swedish), Robert Burns, Walter Von der Vogelweide, Lorca, and, somewhat controversially, Edgar Allen Poe.

There are regular competitions between poets to get into the club: Goethe faced off with Schiller; Baudelaire whipped Victor Hugo's butt; W. B. Yeats is rumored to have bribed someone. As the voting is telepathic, results are known instantly by everyone. I cannot wait to see this place: I really can't.

I have never been the same since I tuned in to a performance of 'Where Have All the Flowers Gone?' by Marlene Dietrich in front of a packed, appreciative crowd. This is, undoubtedly, the jewel in the crown of my EVP recordings. If you thought her voice was husky and sensual when alive, you should hear it in the Afterlife, unmediated by air, and undiluted by vocal chords: it is absolutely mind-blowing, and I weep for joy each time I play it, which is often.

Add to this the chance to sit in the lap of Helen of Troy, take Van Gogh's painting workshop, have piano lessons with Beethoven (which I wouldn't necessarily advise), learn (a little late) about the Universe from Einstein, and listen to Accountants and Archaeologists trying to justify their existence, and you will begin to understand what a wonderful world the Next One is, and how mad you are if you still fear death.

You really won't want to leave this place. Unless you were an Artist though, you will have to. And that is what I will talk about now.

Thank you for coming with me so far, and staying the course. Give yourself a little hug. The real journey is about to begin.

Chapter Five

THE REAL JOURNEY BEGINS

One 'day,' without warning, you begin your journey to God, and embark on Death Phase II. There is a blast of a trumpet. You gather in the company of souls you have been reunited with, or ones you have just met on the Indeterminate Plane. An irresistible impulse comes over you, and you glide in an orderly fashion towards the Astral Dome, which is about 2,000 light years away. A feeling of exaltation builds within.

Twenty-four Angels appear. They are, like all Angels, hermaphrodites, and eight-foot-two-inches tall. They point towards the Astral Dome, and smile. All the souls assembled find themselves moving effortlessly towards it. It's like being on a conveyor belt, without the negative implications of being mass produced.

You move without expending any energy – indeed, from now on, you never expend energy because then it would have to be replaced and you are now completely and eternally self-sustaining.

The twenty-four Angels use the journey to telepathically explain to you how to prepare to meet God and how to behave. You don't need to bow, or courtesy, or think of something clever to catch his attention; He's heard it all before. You just have to get used to the idea that the audience with God, though transfiguring, will be shorter and even more impersonal than that of the Pope with summer tourists.

There are two things you should do, and one thing you shouldn't, while you're drifting towards the Astral Dome:

1. Pace yourself
2. Contemplate God
3. Don't look down.

PACE YOURSELF

The journey is long; it's important that you take things step by step, one light year at a time. Do not consider the enormous distance you have to cover, but focus on the fact that your journey has started and your goal is therefore nearer in reach: savor each light second, and soon the light minutes, hours, days, months and years will go flashing by unnoticed.

Identify what you still need to work on to get the most out of being a soul, and set yourself realistic goals to achieve this: two of the most useful activities you can indulge in during this period are Telepathy and Self-Propulsion.

Telepathy

Telepathy doesn't come naturally: it can be hard, frustrating work. When you send your first messages, I can guarantee they won't be received, or, if they are, they will hit the wrong target, causing endless confusion.

The experienced dead have a lot of fun, and some embarrassment, getting very private messages misdirected to them by incompetent new arrivals. However, since you now have no voice box, and since there is no air in Heaven for sounds to form in, you need to get your telepathic technique up to scratch pretty damn quickly.

From the moment you leave the Indeterminate Zone, use the time to work on your mental annunciation and psychic delivery techniques; practice with a partner, starting with simple, ungrammatical telepathy, and moving on to perfectly formed mind phrases that Shakespeare himself would be – and is – proud of.

Once dead, by the way, Shakespeare became a Doctor of Telepathy in no time at all. His seminars are legendary in the Next World, and souls sigh with pleasure when he wafts his words elegantly towards them.

In the vibrant, vital world of Telepathy the English, I have to say, are, at present the undisputed masters, followed by the Italians and the French. We Americans do ok, but our qualities and priorities – as I explain later – are put to better use elsewhere.

As for Telepathy, Americans, it has to be faced, do get an embarrassingly large portion of our telepathams returned 'undeliverable' or 'incomprehensible.' But, we never give in and we'll get there.

Self-Propulsion

You used to have arms and legs; now you don't. Your ears gave you balance when you moved; now, you're earless. Your eyes showed you where to go, but you left them behind, in your coffin.

Movement in the Next World is a whole new ballgame. It does not come naturally, but through endless training. Much of this was done in the Indeterminate Zone, but few are the souls who have made the most of the propulsive potential of their new Form as they set off to see God. This is by far the most popular pastime of all souls on this journey.

You are moving, irresistibly, towards God, but you are not constrained to keep to the pace and direction set by the Angels, as a sort of ethereal cruise control. You can dip, sway, dive, soar, hover, shoot, stop, sink, float, zip and undulate.

All of this requires practice, and all is accomplished by will-power, whose potential is limitless and endless, and which, in a way, defines your experience in the Afterlife. This, then, must be a beautiful sight, which I can't wait to see for myself: millions of souls moving towards God as one, but deviating, exploring their own potential, perfecting the gifts of Death.

Propulsion by will-power alone is, the dead agree, the single greatest thrill about being dead, especially once you become an expert.

Will-power is also essential to achieve the most from the second main activity I recommend at this stage:

CONTEMPLATE GOD

Think about this: Why would God even want to meet you, you worm? Why would The Creator of Everything even notice you, you pathetic, microscopic parasite?

When you think of the billions of galaxies He has brought into being, the Earth itself is just a speck of dust and you are dust on that dust. And yet, he's called you in for an interview. If this doesn't make you think, nothing ever will. This is scary. This is beyond awesome. This is inconceivable.

How can any preparation be adequate? How on earth can you make a favorable impression? Relax. You can't. Nothing you can do can ever impress God.

What so many have failed to realize is that He's not looking to be impressed. He has His own agenda, which has never before been revealed.

The interview you have with God is unusual, first because it's with God, and second, because you are not required, or allowed, to say anything. Oh, and third: it's not really an interview.

By this, I mean it is not going to be like all those interviews you had on Earth for all those jobs you never got, when such things seemed to matter. It is not a test. It is going to be short, and one-way, but doesn't have to be disappointing. All this is discussed in more detail in Chapter Seven.

For the time being, just as you would research the character and aspirations of the CEO of a Company you want to work for, so will a little practical contemplation of who God actually is go a long way to putting you at your ease when you enter the Astral Dome.

Let's start with the basics: first of all, being dead, you are not as far removed from God as you may think. You have already met the most important requisite for seeing Him: physical decay.

God is Light, and you yourself are now light, so the meeting is on a much more equal footing than during that terrible time when your soul was entombed in your body. Your soul is pure, eternal light, begotten, not made.

Imagine how it felt during all those shameful corporal years, deafened by the thumping of your heart, appalled by the contents of your colon, shocked by your sexual obsessions and blinded by the never-ending waves of false light pitilessly striking your retina.

Let's face it, life on Earth was Hell for your soul. To make it bearable, your soul tried, from time to time, to contemplate and understand God, its only friend, but the senses inevitably ruined the picture, as adolescents draw moustaches on posters of the Mona Lisa. All our portraits of God look stupid, precisely because He's been drawn by idiots.

So, as you make this journey, to finally meet and know God, I say this: don't visualize; remove all preconceptions; strip bare the false images that your fallible mind deceived you with whenever the word 'God' disturbed its contemptible circuits.

He does not have a white beard; He is not vengeful; He is not, thank goodness, your father. He is not a He, certainly not a She, and definitely not an It.

God is not, in fact, in language at all, but the good news is neither are you, when you are dead. This, as I've touched on before, is the problem with writing a book about Him. Words, words, words.

Mediums will understand what I'm talking about. These wonderful, selfless seers are incredibly frustrated at having to use language to communicate to us what the dead reveal to them in meta-form.

Mediums so love the world that they give themselves up freely and without fear to cynical, skeptical abuse. The dead sense mediums as one of them, and communicate in dead-speak, which is a thrill to hear, but a pain in the ass to fully understand.

I am not a medium – I need technology to help me – and the dead respond to me grudgingly, in language. The messages mediums get are, in a sense, more authentic than mine, but sadly untranslateable. This explains the all-too-familiar scenarios published on YouTube with glee by bitter, shallow skeptics:

"I'm getting the word Rob…no, Bob….no, Knob… any Knobs here?"

This is not the medium floundering, or trying to trick you: it is the medium trying to reproduce, as faithfully as possible in language, the FEELING the dead are putting in their psyche.

We've tried for thousands of years to put feelings into words, and you need only open that drawer and look at that poem you once thought was so good to understand what a disaster this generally turns out to be. Anything worth knowing, as all dead souls and psychics know, is inarticulable.

What I'm trying to say is that your soul will not be afraid. God is Light and you are light. He will glow, and you will glimmer. He will speak, and you will be silent. He will see you, and you will see Him. What more could you possibly ask?

I conclude this chapter with a common problem — fear of flying — which causes many people to worry unnecessarily about whether they will get sick in the next world, where floating and flying are so much more the norm:

What To Do on High, When you Hate Heights.

When you went to the Grand Canyon, you thought you had seen it all. The Grand Canyon, my friend, is a peanut compared to what you will see in the next world.

In life, you finally made that 'death defying' bungee jump, and boasted about it for weeks to colleagues and friends. Well, think for a moment: what will you do in Heaven, where there's nowhere to stand, and you have no legs to stand on?

Bungee jump off Mount Everest, if you can find a rope long enough. It cannot prepare you in any way for the journey to meet God, when you are dangling for 2,000 years over a depthless abyss.

There is, because of the logistics of coping with the endless daily arrival of hordes of newly dead souls, quite literally nothing between the Indeterminate Zone and the Astral dome, and you have to float continually over it, maintaining equilibrium and good cheer.

Have you really ever thought carefully about this? An everlasting life of flying and floating with no harness attached, even for those who get nauseous looking down from a second floor balcony? A life of the spirit, where you are always on high, and there's nowhere to sit down, and nothing to sit down with?

I know that those of you who have a fear of heights will, quite understandably, be anxious at the moment. How the hell, you may be thinking, are you, who never dared go on the tamest of roller coasters, going to cope with the vertiginous challenges of being a spirit? That is a reasonable question.

When you are dead, you become a beam of light. Light travels at 700 million miles an hour. How are you going to become a well-adjusted spirit if, on Earth, you got car sick at 30 mph?

Don't worry, the answer, as always, is simple: Vertigo is a preparation for Eternity.

I'll explain. You know that feeling you get when you are standing on the edge of a precipice: that perverse mixture of "I'm going to faint with fear," and "Wouldn't it be interesting to jump?'

Vertigo is, in fact, like so many other 'everyday' experiences, a preparation for the Afterlife. It is your soul flexing its wings, and reminding the body just who's the boss in this partnership.

Your soul wants you to jump – because it likes flying and knows it won't die, whereas your body, knowing it will die, and not yet being adapted to flight, advises you not to.

Calling this conflict 'vertigo' is a bit of an insult. It is much more than physical – as indeed everything is – it is one of the many spiritual learning opportunities we seldom make use of while alive. The soul is showing off.

You could even say it is taunting the body: it is reminding the body that the flesh is weak and, though the body might think it is in charge at the moment, its death will set the soul free. The soul, in exultation, is savoring its future freedom, and trying to tell you everything will be ok once we are stripped bare of this pain-in-the-ass flesh to which it is resentfully attached.

Some of us learn the lesson quickly, some of us don't, depending on who is the dominant partner in our particular marriage of body and soul. The more your body tries to shout down the soul, the more vertigo you will feel.

Not that I'm telling you to jump. The reactions of both parties are correct, and understandable. Our body wants to stay alive as long as possible, because it only gets this one shot; our soul doesn't give a damn about death, because the death of the soul is inconceivable.

There's more chance of me making love to Jennifer Lopez than there is of death entering my soul.

So, to summarize: to those of you who are afraid to fly, and are therefore apprehensive about spending eternity doing nothing but this, your least favorite activity, I say simply: look beneath this fear and listen to your soul, created for endless flight, imprisoned in a mortal body.

Enjoy your body while you can, but, as you reach the point of no return, listen more to your soul, voicing its natural, heartfelt complaint about the indignity of being forced to reside near so many base, corruptible organs: Every single soul in every single human being ever created has, at one time or another, cried out loud in agony: "Let me out! It stinks in here!"

And, when you're dead and crossing the Abyss, in the unlikely event that your soul is still tainted with remnants of vertigo, if you feel nausea coming on, as you did on Earth, so you should do in Heaven: don't look down.

The journey is long but, like all journeys, it has an end, and now the Astral Dome is clearly in sight. You may see God very soon or, in keeping with the total freedom you now enjoy, you actually may not. There is, at this late stage, a potential detour.

Chapter Six

WHEN THINGS GO WRONG

There is a fork in the road as you approach the Astral Dome which, if taken, may lead to destruction. It appears before you, as you round a bend and glimpse, for the first time, the magnificence of the edifice where God himself will meet you.

The fork veers off to the left, and can lead to absolute darkness. Take this left turn, and you may never see God. I repeat: those who go left, those who are even tempted to see what life is like on the left side may never see God. Not for nothing is the word for 'left' in Latin 'sinister.' The left is sinister; the left hand is sinister; what some people do with their left hand is very sinister indeed.

God is to the right. Always has been; always will be. End of story.

Ninety percent of souls who see the Astral Dome at this point do not hesitate: they turn right and march towards it, fearlessly and confidently, as we Americans used to until very recently. Two percent of the remainder sit down at the fork and don't know what to do; it may be the equivalent of days, months, years or millennia before they finally make up their mind.

Here, dear Reader, I'm afraid, is where you may well find me. I am, I now confess, incapable of making a decision. I blame it on being only half American. My mother is Irish – by which I mean she really was born in Ireland. No doubt I get from her the creative insight to write a book, but my God, it hasn't half held up my career in other ways.

My dad is from the Bronx, and from him I get my dominant, scientific impulse. Should you die after me, arrive at this spiritual crossroads, and see me sitting there with a vacant expression on my face, please come up to me, remind me I wrote this book, and give me a kick up the backside so I may go on. I will thank you, in the end.

As for the remaining 8%, they look at the brilliant purity of the Dome, consider for a moment, the pros and cons of meeting up with God, shrug their shoulders, and go left, into the potential darkness.

What happens to these lefties? Are they punished? Are they deluded? What if you are one of them? What should you do, when you see a vision of glory to your right, and a little, devilish voice inside whispers, "Go left, and see what happens?"

Remember what we have learned so far: there is no Hell, therefore no punishment. No immortal soul, strictly speaking, can be called 'deluded.' You are perfectly within your rights, as a Free Spirit, to see God's Glory in the distance, shake your head, and say: "No thanks." If you do make this choice, here's what to expect.

The road left itself splits into three paths, clearly signposted in red, blue and white. The red signpost leads to a red tunnel; the blue signpost leads to a blue tunnel, and so on.

The red tunnel is taken by those who feel cheated that there is no Hell, and wish to experience what punishment might have felt like, had Hell existed; these are commonly, if inaccurately, called masochists. The blue tunnel leads straight back to Earth and is for those so-called sadists, who have what I call '*Wuthering Heights* Syndrome' and think they miss the Earth.

These two tunnels are potentially just temporary detours: you eventually emerge on the other side, hopefully satisfied, and ready at last to meet God. In each of them, however, just before you emerge, there is a short cut to the white tunnel, for those who change their minds.

The white tunnel is completely different: those who take the white tunnel are irredeemable, and will experience complete and permanent oblivion. I am not joking: complete and permanent oblivion.

Before I take you down each separate road, let me make something clear. When it comes to making choices, as it is on the earth, so it is in Heaven: follow your heart. You have had a taste of eternity up to now; here is where you either drain it to the last drop, or throw away the cup.

Don't worry about hurting God's feelings: it is not disrespectful to God to reject him forever: in fact, you are using his gift of Free Will purposely and, in a sense, exactly as it was intended. Life is a gift, and, contrary to popular opinion, how you use that gift is a matter of some indifference to the Deity. It is a poor friend indeed who gives you a shirt as a Christmas present, then angrily takes it back a year later because you couldn't be bothered to wear it.

The Red Tunnel

Some souls have read so much about Hell that they feel the need to experience it themselves. They feel that eternity would not be complete unless you felt, for a moment, eternal pain.

As in many other cases, Dante is chiefly to blame. 80% of souls who want to go to Hell have read Dante's *Inferno* with great pleasure, but found *Purgatorio* and *Paradiso* hard going. They identify with Francesca the Adulteress, Brunetto the Gay, Brutus the Friend-Killer, Pier the Self-Destructive, or sometimes Satan himself. They are under the delusion that you can't have Heaven without Hell. They ask for grief, and it is given.

God, in fact, has done a great job in supplying this experience, without actually damning you forever. If you choose this path, here is what happens.

There are black carriages outside the red tunnel waiting to take you in. They are driven by skeletons, headless horsemen, foul-smelling goblins, and mice. The carriage itself stinks of vomit, diapers and broccoli.

The music that you hated most in life is played continually to you once you are in your seat. This will play non-stop, until you finally beg for release. Imagine listening to Frank Zappa forever and ever. Even if you like Frank Zappa.

The carriage jerks forward a few meters, and you stop suddenly to read this sign, which is unfortunately too long to fit on this page:

(continued)

ENTER WITH HORROR THE LAND OF JAMMAJANNA

HERE YOU WILL FIND THE PAIN OF ENDLESS CHILDBIRTH,

THE NAUSEA OF HAVING YOUR HEAD HELD IN AN ETERNAL TOILET CLOGGED WITH DIARRHEA,

THE CEASELESS SOUND OF FINGERNAILS ON A BLACKBOARD,

RATS WHO CRAWL FOREVER INTO YOUR EYESOCKETS AND EAT THE JELLY OF YOUR EYES.

ALL OF THIS AND MORE YOU WILL EXPERIENCE.

JAMMAJANNA IS WHERE YOU GET YOUR BODY BACK, AND WISH TO GOD YOU HADN'T.

JAMMAJANNA IS SELF-INFLICTED TORMENT.

JAMMAJANNA IS PAIN.

YOU ASKED FOR IT, SO HERE IT IS.

LEAVE HOPE AT THE ENTRANCE, AND MAY IT BE THERE TO MEET YOU ON YOUR WAY OUT.

P.S:
JAMMAJANNA IS NOT FOREVER: IT IS MERELY DESIGNED TO FEEL SO.

PRESS THE GREEN BUTTON WHEN YOU HAVE SUPPED FULL OF HORROR.

You are allowed time to digest this information, and asked if you have changed your mind before you go on; most say no, and wave the carriage imperiously forward. The carriage moves on, and into the Almost-Hell. However cocky you felt before, you soon regret it.

The first thing that happens is that your body falls – clomp! – out of nowhere, onto your soul. No shock could be greater. You have been used to being boundless and pure, now you are stuck in flesh again. It's horrible. You even have your penis and/or vagina back: not to feel the thrill of sex, but to experience the agony of a full bladder that can never be emptied, and eternal menstruation.

Knives come out of walls at random, stab you, and the blood cannot be staunched. You ride past a huge bucket, towering above you, like they have in water parks all over the world, but, when this one tips up, it's full of shit.

Rats are released, and climb into your eye sockets. Straps appear, wrap themselves around your legs and pull your legs apart. From this moment, women experience simultaneously the excruciating agony of childbirth, and the worst period of their life, with no epidural, no tampon, and no baby at the end. As for the men in this position, small, spiral-shaped pieces of sharp metal appear at the bottom of the carriage, and work their way towards your scrotum, your rectum, and your penis, burrowing their way slowly and expertly into each.

What more can I say? You go in there with a swagger, but after five minutes, sometimes just seconds, you're pushing that green button like a madman, begging to be released.

The current record for enduring Jammajanna is three hours and five seconds, set by the Marquis de Sade. The shortest time spent in Jammajanna is 0.000003 of a second, set by Sir Terence Wallingford, a Conservative Member of Parliament from Guildford, UK.

As soon as that button is pressed, you find yourself instantaneously transported out of Jammajanna, out of your body, ready and eager to meet God. There is a feeling of redemption and rebirth and, though some now contemplate Oblivion, 96% of souls head directly to the Dome, singing and elated. The songs are various odes to Joy; the most popular song of redemption goes like this, to the tune of *When The Saints Go Marching In:*

> *We've tasted Shit*
> *(We've tasted Shit)*
> *We've tasted Shit*
> *But now we're pure*
> *And since we know what shit tastes like*
> *We ain't gonna eat no shit no more.*
> *(repeat)*

The Blue Tunnel

"Heaven did not seem to be my home; and I broke my heart with weeping to come back to earth; and the angels were so angry that they flung me out, into the middle of the heath, on the top of Wuthering Heights.'"

I've always found this passage by Emily Brontë inspiring and perplexing; inspiring, because it is clearly the result of Astral Projection: Emily, probably while asleep, or perhaps while staring out of the parsonage window, as she often did, has tapped into the real life experience of countless dead souls and exposed the reality of the Blue tunnel 160 years before I was able to confirm it.

The passage is also puzzling because Angels do not get angry, and certainly don't fling you into the blue tunnel – you drift in of your own accord. Moreover, there is something disquieting about a soul falling from Heaven and landing on the roof of a house in Yorkshire, as Kathy does. Is that where she is meant to be? Surely she would be much better off inside Wuthering Heights, rather than perched precariously on the slates?

Anyway, I'm not a literary critic, and I haven't had the good luck to talk to Emily Brontë (which I'd dearly love to do), so I suppose I will have to wait until I die to ask her why she wrote this as she did.

The important thing for you to know is that Emily Brontë has got the essentials right: Souls *are* allowed to return to Earth, if they miss it so much, and they can stay as long as they wish and not, as others have claimed, just for a fortnight on an invisible travelers visa.

Souls who wish to return to Earth are generally those who did not make full use of their psychic abilities and multisensory perception while alive, and feel a little ashamed of this once they die.

Have you ever not been thinking about an old friend when the phone suddenly rings and a voice on the other end tells you he is dead? You could be a candidate for a return to Earth. Had you been properly tuned in to your soul, you would have known the instant he died.

Souls are inter-connected, on a personal, national, international, universal and, ultimately eternal basis. They are all divine, so how could it be otherwise? It takes some of us so long to see this while alive. There is a higher form of reasoning, which is constantly blocked and interfered with by rational thought, the mortal enemy of spiritual progress.

You'll be amazed how little rational thought is needed once you die. As a scientist, I used to be appalled at how sloppily mathematics – and indeed, everything – is taught in America. Now, I'm not so sure. Perhaps the Universe is finally unfolding right here, guiding us in the right direction, away from thought, teaching us the tremendous lessons of the soul, that we are all potential psychics, that intuition is the only real source of knowledge, that hard work is often a waste of time, and that mathematics probably is just for nerds.

I say this even as a scientist, because I have come to understand that there is a higher force than science on the Earth. There is a force called the World Spirit, which is more alive than you are.

It is the Soul of the World, and goes where Civilization advances. It stayed for quite some time in Greece, Rome, China, and Great Britain, and made brief trips to

Italy, France and Spain. For the last two centuries, though, the World Spirit has been living exclusively in America. Throughout our time as the Soul of the World, what we have done to rational thought cannot be a coincidence.

As you might expect, when you look at the attendance statistics for these three tunnels, though Hell and Oblivion are of interest to many Americans, we leave this, the Blue one, to those whose nature is to look back, such as The British, The Irish, and the Canadian.

The White Tunnel

The soul cannot be destroyed, but it can be sent to Oblivion. The word 'oblivion' comes from the Latin 'obliviscor,' which means 'to forget.' The soul can be made to forget who it is, like your grandmother after a few gins, the difference being that obliviscation of the soul is permanent, irreversible, and not to be entered into lightly.

To understand the process, you need a rudimentary understanding of what the soul is made of. Strictly speaking, it is not made of anything, but, for now, it is best described as self-comprehending light. All that happens is that the self-comprehending part is switched off. Not destroyed, but permanently switched off. As far as I understand it, once you emerges from the white tunnel, the light remains but there's no-one at home, as it were.

Such processed souls are then sent to a kind of museum in the Indeterminate Zone, where they hang perpetually motionless, and are the subject of heated debate and endless controversy, none of which they hear or care about.

People who opt for the white tunnel fall into three distinct groups: Atheists with an irredeemable chip on their shoulders, suicide bombers who couldn't believe there were no virgins at the end of the tunnel, and college professors of English who went untenured to their graves.

There are other, isolated soul types, not easy to categorize who also choose to end it all. The most famous of these, I'm reliably informed, is Greta Garbo, who craved solitude in the Afterlife as much as she had in this one, and saw Oblivion as the only way to avoid the hordes of dead autograph hunters who pestered her all the time. She went to Oblivion, they say, without a word, and so became a legend in the next world, as well as this one.

All of these souls harbor vestiges of what can only be called pride, but it is to God's eternal credit that He delights in the positivity of those souls who reject Him. Once you are dead, you cannot doubt anymore that God exists, but you still can say 'so what?'

This is a wonderful gift. Those who choose this path see it themselves as a dynamic expression of their particular view of creation and show a touching solidarity as they march towards extinction.

There is a popular song souls sing on the road to Oblivion, to the tune of 'The Battle Hymn of the Republic' which explains their position better than I can:

I just can't seem to join in all those songs about The Lord
He invented Homo Sapiens one day when he was bored
He gave us Sex; He gave us Soul; He cut the cosmic Chord
Now we've nowhere to be moored!
I'm not going to see God ever!
I'm not going to see God ever!
I'm not going to see God ever!
It's my eternal choice!

This song reverberates throughout this zone, and can be heard faintly but distinctly back at the Astral crossroads themselves. The song dies down, and voices fade as the actual white tunnel itself suddenly looms out of the darkness, like an iceberg before the *Titanic*.

It is pure white, inside and out, and immensely high. It is fifty thousand times bigger than one of those post-modernist tubes that French Architects stuck onto the Georges Pompidou Centre in Paris in the 1970s.

The dead are struck dumb with awe at the sight. This is their moment of truth, and they know it. There are rows of sober soul counselors waiting on either side of the path as you approach.

At first, from afar, they seem like flying or hovering ants but, as you draw near, you see they are simply dark-suited Angels, with kind, intelligent faces. It is a condition of being allowed the privilege to incinerate your soul that you agree to talk to a soul counselor first.

These counselors are well trained and do not try to persuade you one way or the other; they simply remind you of what you are doing, ensure you are aware of what extinction means.

I was immensely lucky to catch the conversation between a soul counselor and Eric Morris, who sounds to me as if he were a Social Worker when he had a body.

I made this precious recording in my early days as a researcher and I recorded the conversation, not at my Spiritual HQ in Toms River, where they have state-of-the-art technology, but in my kitchen, quite by chance. I noticed my cat JJ was staring at the wall, with wide, uncomprehending eyes. This is always a hopeful sign that something paranormal is at work, so I turned on my EVP recorder. The ethereal intercourse monitor was moving more than usual, in a pattern I had never seen before. I watched it for a while, turned on the interface microphone, and called out, "Is anybody there?"

I got, as was usual in those days, no response whatsoever. I should tell you that, in those days, I was still using one of the earlier, non-interactive EVP detectors that now seem as quaint as a CD player. I laugh now to think that it didn't even have Dolby. You couldn't actually converse with the dead on it, just eavesdrop; nor could you find out what, if anything, you had tuned in to, except by playing it back laboriously later.

How many hours I devoted, in those primitive, bygone days, to listening to white noise. Try listening to a blank tape for three weeks non-stop, and see if you can keep your sanity. That is what I used to do on a regular basis, when I first started tracking the Dead and normalizing the paranormal. Yet, believe you me, the thrill of hearing a few seconds of sound from beyond the grave among the hiss of neantise was such that I even regret at times the progress made by Bose and other companies in producing voices from beyond the grave of digital, surround-sound quality.

If you are young, you may not understand. If you are old and have an iPod but still play your LP collection with guilty pleasure, you will.

Anyway, I sensed something was being transmitted, and so I left the recorder on, and went to watch the newly released *Harry Potter and the Chamber of Secrets* at my local movie theater.

When I came back, the tape had finished and the battery had gone dead. I put in a new battery, went upstairs to bed, pressed the play button thinking that the usual white noise would put me to sleep, and seconds later, my heart literally stopped, as this is what I heard:

"Eric Morris?"
"Yes."
"Why do you choose Oblivion over Eternal life?"
"I'm a nihilist."
"You're not attracted to Eternity?"
"No."
"You do not wish to meet God?"
"No."
"You're not afraid?"
"No."
"Do you have any questions?"
"No."

"Do you have any friends you wish to accompany you to the threshold?"
"No."
"In that case, by the power vested in me—"
"*IS ANYBODY THERE?*"
"What the Hell?!"

Here, unfortunately, the conversation stopped dead. Perhaps it was the shock of my voice coming through at this most personal of moments, or maybe they moved to a quieter spot, out of my electro-magnetic range. I had not thought before how strange it must be, when you are dead, to have a voice from the previous world come out at you through thin air.

Whatever the reason, this recording – one of my most valuable – remains the first and so far only direct evidence that there is choice in the next world, that you are not forced to live forever, or even see God if you don't want to.. Nothing is done against your will. I find that exhilarating.

Many other spirits have since confirmed the existence of the White Tunnel and say that once you have talked to a soul counselor, there is no going back. More than a few of them describe souls who take this option as 'idiots.'

Chapter Seven

WHAT TO DO WHEN YOU FINALLY MEET GOD

*W*e now come to the most breakthrough part of this guide. No other book has told you in such simple terms what it will be like to meet God, how you should behave and, most important of all, how to cope with the depression that all too often sets in once you finally meet the Creator of the Universe, and all you get out of him is one word.

Before you meet God, though, it will do no harm at all to know something about him. Previous descriptions have been, at best, little more than informed guesswork. People have believed, through various stages of human history, that god is a warrior, a king, the sun, a dog ('god' spelt backwards), and a tortoise.

EVPs have changed all that. Twenty-four souls that I have recorded have actually met God, among them a learned theologian, called Brother Owens, who puts things into context:

> "What you have to understand about God is that he is ineffable, and therefore gets bored very quickly. Contemplating his own creation was ok for a few billennia; black holes

stirred things up no end, but there was always something missing in his life.

"Finally, he understood what it was: he wasn't having fun. There was no-one to have fun with, for God does not have a significant other. He thought about making one, but it soon became apparent that the one thing he couldn't create was himself: anything he made would *(ipso facto)* be created, and anything created is not God.

"After what seemed like an eternity, he chose the next best thing, which was to put a divine spark, willy-nilly, in all of us. What people – including myself – have failed to grasp is that he did this more to liberate himself than us. He was preparing us to take over, so he could go into semi-retirement and enjoy a much earned rest.

"There are two simple things God has always wanted to do in retirement: play dice with the universe, and have a game of hide-and-go seek. He did not play dice until recently because he knew in advance every number of every dice ever thrown in the now, the was and the will be.

"As for hide-and-go seek, if you are everywhere, as God is, where the hell in the universe can you hide? Imagine you are 'it' and are counting to thirty, while an omnipresent God is scurrying around looking for somewhere He isn't.

"'Damn...damn...damn...damn...damn...' You can almost hear him mutter. 'Ready or not, here I come...oh, there you are! DAMN!'

"If He were to make – as he has done – somewhere where He isn't, all this would change. This is precisely what happens when He meets us; he forsakes us. He loses his capital letter. He tells us a word, and leaves us in darkness."

These revelations by Brother Owens are startling, but confirmed by every spirit who has had this experience. There has been much talk and debate about what the Word is.

I can safely tell you, that despite thousands of years of theological dead ends, that's all it is – a word. Not a word as we would say, or think it, but a word that we recognize as belonging to the time when language made sense.

It is a recollection, a moment in the present, and a foreshadowing of the future. Time present and time past are contained in the word God gives you and, after he's said it, by some mystery of consubstantiality – or, as James Joyce put it, "fuck knows how" – God does actually disappear, and you are on your own forever.

But, what is the experience itself like? This, essentially, is what happens: you find yourself before the pearl-encrusted gate of the Astral Dome. Angels line the entrance, and nod to you as you glide past.

You enter. There is a thrilling radiance of pure energy. You float towards the Source, feel yourself examined, but bathed in a loving light. You hear a voice. The most beautiful voice you have ever heard in your life, or will ever hear. It speaks one word. You want to stop and make the moment last forever, but the conveyor belt goes on. Before you know it, the light has gone, a celestial curtain has closed, and you find yourself outside, in indeterminate darkness. The audience is over, almost before it began, and your most puzzling, but exhilarating adventure is about to begin.

This is the ultimate mystery of the Afterlife. God greets all dead souls with just one word. The word is different for every single soul. What it means is up to you to decide.

A warning: do not be disappointed by the shortness of this conversation. This is the primal cause of Post Deity Depression. The important thing to remember is that God has spoken to you. Be grateful. Think.

He is the Creator of the Universe. The seven billion humans on the surface of our planet account for less than 0.000000000000000000000000001% of His creation. There are trillions more aliens than us and, at the last count, 865 billion religions outside our solar system, all vying for His attention.

Did you, throughout the whole of your life, ever speak to a tadpole? This is what He has done for you. Yet still we wish for more. The ingratitude of the dead can be breathtaking.

What happens when you float towards the Creator of The Universe, and hear Him finally speak? I will let the dead tell you for themselves. First, Jose Penepicolo, a softly spoken teacher of ESL, originally from Venezuela:

> "It was my turn. The light was overwhelming. The source of this light was contained on a pure white throne. I bowed my head. I heard a voice. The most beautiful of voices. It spoke within and without me. What it said was 'Hola.' Then there was silence.

"I thought it was the beginning of a conversation, but it was the end. The throne became as nothing and I was edged gently, irrevocably out of His presence forever. I was...how do you say...bereft.

"I had waited all my life to meet God; I had died; and all he had said was 'Hola.' I could not help but feel a little cheated. 'Was it for this that I lived as a Catholic?' I couldn't help thinking."

James Joyce's voice, soft, calm and forever Irish, is clearer on this tape than on any other.

"What did God say to me? I'll tell you what God said to me: he said 'zinc.'"

"Zinc?" I repeated.

"Zinc."

"What does that mean?" I asked

"God knows," said James Joyce.

This is, I confess, the only part of this book where I cannot help you. I do not understand this part of the journey, but I must faithfully report it.

I have the evidence of 22 other souls who have heard their word; all of them confess to being perplexed, and even haunted, by it. These words, the last they will ever hear, are, in no particular order:

Carbon

Procrastinate

Elephant

Eftsoones

See (Sea?)

Placate

Maybe

Inform

ABBA

Death

Pink

Metempsychosis

The

Yes

Poppins

Perplex

Foment

And

Endless

Love

Silence

Song

This is what will happen one day to you too: your word will be spoken and you will be in the Dark once again. A darkness of Swedish proportions. You are glowing; all other souls are glowing. The trouble is what you are glowing in seems to be nothing. And, it's endless.

Perplexion and sadness at this stage of your journey are perfectly normal. In many ways, though, as I will soon reveal, you are lucky to be dying when you are because things are finally getting sorted out up there, as souls are at last beginning to understand, for the first time in Afterlife history, the divine revelation we have only just cottoned on to.

In short, as the next chapter will finally explain:

There is more to being dead than meeting God.

Chapter Eight

THERE IS MORE TO BEING DEAD THAN MEETING GOD

Let's recap:

- You have died;
- You have been in and out of the tunnel;
- The 21 grams of matter that your soul contained whilst in your body has been transformed into your eternal Form, which is a self-sustaining beam of pure light;
- You need to see God, but He's not the sort of being you just walk in on without an appointment;
- There is ample provision for you to pass the 'time' before you meet God, by visiting the living, improving your spiritual profile, getting used to the idea that you *can* travel at the speed of light (because you *are* light), meeting up with old friends, making new ones and watching dead aliens go their separate paths to their particular Nirvana;
- The Angels have guided you to the Astral Dome (if you are sensible, you probably did not take one of the optional detours);
- You met God, He gave you your word, you've no idea what it means and nobody ever does.

He has forsaken you. You are on your own as never before. Before you died, you thought things would all be worked out for you. All you would have to do is turn up.

How wrong can you be! There is work to be done. There is always work to be done. I will save you a lot of soul-searching – some souls have been searching at this stage for more than three million years – by explaining what has happened.

First of all, remember you are an American. Your country brought optimism and democracy into the world. God loves your country, above all others. He has a plan. You have the energy and resourcefulness to understand that plan and implement it.

Americans never give up: we are One Nation, United under God: from the aging call-girls in the Bronx, to the hallowed head of the Disney Corporation in L.A, we are one and the same, with a special destiny to fulfill God's mission.

God has heard 'God Bless America' a billion times since it was first composed. Do you think for one moment he has stopped listening? Hell, no. There is a reason, that no-one has hitherto suspected, why America is great and I am about to reveal it.

First of all, a word about Divine Revelation, and why it has been so often misinterpreted in pre-American history. God has desperately been sending us revelations since time immemorial. They are always simple.

But human beings have not been simple enough to understand them until the twentieth century, when

America became Number One, when we knocked all forms of unnecessary thought – the abstract, the complicated the sustained and the multi-layered – out of the ball-park once and for all, and God cried, "Hallelujah!" People had been thinking far too much for far too long. Then God gave America independence.

Divine revelation is not rocket science: it can be seen in the simplest human act. Think of a teenage girl, in New Jersey, during a high school Spanish lesson, blowing bubble gum. This is not a waste of time. This act is a divinely inspired allegory of Creation. The bubble gum is a blue collar Big Bang. God is demonstrating, through her, for those who have eyes to see, the mystery of Creation.

In the beginning, He, too, took a small particle, popped it into His mouth, swirled it around for a while, and blew. The Universe emerged, expanding more or less uniformly through the power of God's breath, always away from the source.

God's breath is infinite, but the gum we are made of, alas, is not. It has its breaking point. This is reached, in the case of gum, three to twelve seconds after creation, depending on the girl's blowing experience, and lung capacity.

With the Universe, it lasts a little longer: some say four thousand years; others say eight hundred and fifty two thousand three hundred and twelve billion. The actual figure, I believe, is somewhere in between.

What is certain is that we, the Universe, will pop. This is not God's fault. Nor is it a deficiency: when you blow gum, the explosion and the implosion are equally exciting. The beginning and end are uniformly rewarding, for God and for Creation. We are starbursts.

And, the good news is, the gum is never destroyed. Just like the girl, God pops it back into his mouth, swirls it round, and begins again. Even when it gets tasteless, even when the gum is ejected to the floor, stays splattered there, or sticks to someone's shoe, this is not evidence of a deficiency. Such gum is the stuff that parallel universes are made of.

And – this is the important bit – the true entrance to Eternity, which opens after you've met god, is precisely this: a parallel, godless world made of spiritual Gum that was, but now isn't, God.

God finally found a way to stick it to our shoe, and disclaim responsibility. Now and forever, the place where you are will always be precisely the place he is not.

All the dead who have come this far confirm that, after you've seen God and left the celestial Astrum, a portal to endless darkness opens, which you enter with some reluctance.

You must go through this Portal; it is the end of the beginning and is only scary for those who wanted to be comfortable in the next life. Eternity is not about comfort, it is about getting on with the job in hand. It is about complete detachment from everything you ever believed.

To help you in this detachment process, before you go through this portal, you get a vision of the future: a vision of the dying Earth. This is your final lesson in the finite. It is not meant to depress, but invigorate you and leave you to face what humans try not to think about: cosmic loneliness.

You are alone, but this is a reward, not a punishment. The lesson is simple: step out of your narrow, terrestrial box: leave behind the comfort zone in which the word 'home' entraps us: the earth is not your home; you cannot have a home, if you want to be like God.

Furthermore, in order to be like God, you must become like a little child, and rebel against your parents. Seeing the Earth die is the first step on this final journey, which is endless.

The Earth does not go out in a blaze of glory. It dies a slow, sad death, as it is stripped remorselessly bare of life: trees and grass and mountains and meadows and oceans just disappear. There is no more water, no more blue sky, no human or animal movement whatsoever.

All planets, like ourselves, will one day become mere corpses and, after it has died, the Earth turns helplessly in space for a while, like a dead leaf on a dying breeze, until, finally, it returns to dust. Where it used to be is unrecorded, but the Universe goes on.

"The Universe is amazing," you think, "but there's no point to it whatsoever." And it occurs to the dead at this stage that the life you lived was a meaningless gift from someone you barely knew.

And, once you have grasped this, Revelation is not far behind.

Chapter Nine

HAPPY EVER AFTER

*G*od is behind you, where he always wanted to be. There is no more space; time has ceased to be; the stars have disappeared; the planets have disappeared; light has disappeared. Nowhere and Somewhere are the same. No wonder you have a headache.

To have come this far, and be shut out of a celestial banquet, with darkness stretching endlessly before you, seems, at first, to be a downer.

Souls from Sweden have the most difficulty coping with this situation. They haven't been able to go forward since the Crusades, and thus it is they who suffer most from Post Deity Depression. Bjorn Thorson, with whom I have had many enlightening talks, is the source of this information.

> "We Swedes, you know, are miserable bastards. Ours is a dark country: from the age of five, we are forced to watch movies by Ingmar Bergman, which does not help our in-built suicidal tendencies. And look what happens when we do try to break out of depression: bloody ABBA.

> "Min Gud, when I came out of that Astral Dome, the only place I had ever felt true warmth and happiness, when that gate slammed shut, and absolute blackness lay ahead, I thought I was back in Stockholm. Worst of all, here, on the threshold of Eternity, I was surrounded by fellow Swedes, who were too tired, too miserable, or too apathetic to go on. It was a hard, hard time, but then..."

But then! Ah, but then! We are coming to the end of our journey. I – and God – have saved the best till last.

What happens to these poor Nordics? What, if anything, gives them the impulse to break out of this black despair?

Here's the best news of all: We do! Americans, with our boundless energy and optimism, were the first to make that leap into the dark, and reveal the eternal wonder behind it.

The Truth, as always, is very simple: When we are shown the Celestial Door, we come face to face with the Ultimate Spiritual Truth: Dark Matter.

Do you know your physics? If not, Google "Dark Matter" now to save me the time of explaining to you what it is thought to be. You only need the crassest of explanations, so Wikipedia will do.

There you will find that Dark Matter accounts for 95% of the Universe and is all about WIMPS (Weakly Interacting Massive Particles). Quantum Physicists know Dark Matter exists, but don't know what it is, or what it is for.

I do. I have been told what it is by the Dead, for they are up to their necks in it. Fabio Cazzato, a Catholic graduate of MIT explained it most clearly:

> "Now that I am dead, I fully understand why God made The Universe such a gloomy and soulless place. 'Let there be Light' is a bit misleading: the fact is that, in the Beginning, God said 'Let there be Light!' and there was 95% darkness.

> "This is what my colleagues identified as Dark Matter shortly before I died in that unfortunate experiment. But, what, exactly is Dark Matter? Dark Matter has been compared to Dennis Rodman: sad, scary and the end of life as we know it. It is nothing of the kind.

> "Dark Matter was created for our spiritual salvation. Each dead soul, once he has seen God, is given a particle of Dark Matter to play with, until they figure out how to make it as light as they are.

> "I believe the Word you are given by God is a spiritual spade to dig into the darkness. No soul has managed this task yet, but incredible progress has been made since an independent America was born, which, in turn, allowed independent Americans to start dying.

> "When souls finally manage to transform Dark Matter, they will enter a new Eternity and understand God, for they too will have said 'Let there be Light!' and there will be Light. We will finally become what God wants us all to become: minigods, and God himself can wash us out of his hair, as it were.

> "What no religion has yet understood is that you cannot be totally free until you are free from God. God understood this. Dark Matter is the final piece in His jigsaw. Each particle of Dark Matter will be put to good use in the salvation of us all. As with everything else, God foresaw this. Now, if you will excuse me, I have some digging to do."

"God foresaw this." Unfortunately, until relatively recently, we didn't. Dead souls – even Socrates, Genghis Khan and St Peter – felt abandoned in the dark.

They were not unhappy, but they thought that they had landed in a peculiar Paradise. They did not realize that they had entered a portal back to the Universe to complete God's work, by creating Light from Darkness, so that Man could once and for all lift the weight of the Universe off God's broad but restless shoulders.

Now, at last, we begin to understand the History of the Dead, and why being dead has been, until now, so relatively uneventful. Under the conditions of Free Will, it is not God's job to explain things to us. When you are dead, it is up to you to work out why.

So, after meeting them and giving them their word, God left the dead in Dark Matter from day one without explanation.

And there they stayed, from the death of our common mother Lucy 3 million years ago, until October 18th 1931, that momentous day when Thomas Edison finally died, and entered the Next World armed with intelligence, and a flashlight.

Whatever you say about Edison, he wasn't afraid of the Dark. He is, more than any Pope, the Champion of Light. During his brief stay on Earth, he made 9,000 defective light bulbs before he finally got one to work. He was made in America, and, more than any soul in History, made to confront Dark Matter. Edison it was who first, over four score years ago, rolled up his metaphorical sleeves, understood there is work to be done when you die, and planted an American flag in the virginal Darkness.

You should have been there to hear those lusty American cheers when, under Edison's guiding touch, Dark Matter first began to get a silver lining. America's Destiny is greater than even you, my friend, can imagine. God himself had been praying for someone like Edison to come along and claim this negatively charged New World, and now that we have, there's no looking back or dilly-dallying anymore.

American souls were the first to put their backs into Dark Matter, to recognize its real potential, and use it to build a *new* New World, for the benefit of all Mankind. Even as I speak, an American-led Consortium of Souls is edging Dark Matter into Light at such a speed that – I can confidently predict – by the summer of 2114, when scientists train their powerful telescopes onto that cold, black void, for the first time in History, the living will be able to see, and wave to, the dead at work.

Soon after that, the Dead and the Living will be as one, the *new* New World will begin, and, in gratitude to the spirit of Thomas Edison, its founder, the language spoken by all for all Eternity will be American English.

Much follows from this. Human History finally begins to make sense: its sole purpose has been to produce the USA. God willed the USA into being to deal a death blow to abstract thought, so that when Edison died, practical American souls would rally around him to unclog the system that was trapping the unenlightened, un-American Dead.

My fellow Americans, in these dark, uncertain days, this is my Good News to you all: America has taken charge of the Next World. The pioneer spirit that saw us shake off the shackles of England sees us thrive once more in this ultimate of God-given tasks.

This New Land is Our Land: this black, unending darkness, which should terrify the intelligent, has no effect whatsoever on us! Our God-given sense of boundless possibility, our refusal to be beaten down, our healthy suspicion (and complete lack) of thought, shines like a beacon to weaker, more hesitant souls.

We embrace eternal darkness with joy, and every immortal soul follows us with gratitude. Let there be Light! Oh, my Word! If you could see what I see as I write this! Extraordinary things are happening in the Great Beyond as a result of Edison, and this courage of ours! We hug those hapless Swedes, and black despair falls from them, like underwear from their favorite fantasy; we laugh, and a new kind of light appears; we work as one Nation under Death, and brand new stars are created; we are positive, and negativity bows its hopeless, rational head.

As we Americans blaze the trail, the realization of what Eternity is dawns on all the dead: we are all Creators now; the darkness before us is not a punishment, it is Infinite Possibility, to shape in whatever way we like, without god's interference. And, for the first time in his long life, God can – and has – put his feet up.

So, this is what dead souls who have seen God are doing as I speak: shaping a new type of reality that god will never lay claim to.

This is why America grew so rapidly in such a short space of time: to fill the Next World with an increasingly large quota of American souls. We are needed now in that world, perhaps even more than we are needed in this one.

Can you, too, live this way, without God? Can you take his place, and manage an empty, eternal void without him? Yes, you can!

And if you fear death, if you think you will become nothing, if you have the slightest doubt about Eternity, think again, and, the next time you think you're trapped in a hole in New Jersey, look up, and look out, as I do, and you too, my friend will see billions of dead souls, led by Edison himself, cheerful in an Abyss, planting a small seed of light in the seemingly infinite Darkness.

About the Author

John Farquhar was born in England, and educated at Liverpool University and St. John's College, Oxford. He left Oxford quite some time ago for New Jersey, where he earns a modest-but-respectable living as a literature professor, talking passionately to students about dead people and their imaginary friends.

John has adapted just fine to life in America, and now cheerfully answers any questions about his bowel movements and sex life posed to him by complete strangers. Although a traditionalist at heart, he does not use the old-fashioned finger to communicate disaffection with his fellow New Jersey drivers, but prefers the post-modern thumbs up, whose irony and ambiguity he finds much more intellectually satisfying.

Acknowledgements

I would like to thank Amy Hollinger and all the staff at *Hypothetical Press* for believing in this book. On reading my little manuscript, others said: "what the hell is this?" Amy alone said: "what the hell…"

To the members of The South Jersey Writers' Group who laughed, or at least smiled, when I first read out extracts of this book, thank you. You gave me the hope that lunacy is the new normal, and that no lunatic is ever truly alone. I am thinking in particular of Marie Gilbert, Kitty Bergeron, Dawn Byrne, Barbara Godshalk, Jord Fox, Victoria Lees, William Harden, Krista Magrowski, Bob Cook, Patti O'Brien, and Glenn Walker, that wonderful guy with the french fries blog.

I would like to thank Chris Fitter, Rafey Habib and Chris Lightfoot for years and years and years of friendship. Southmoor Rd forever….

To Emma Vanazzi: Thank you for being a friend. Where are the snows of Adelaide Street?

To my family in England: (G)god bless you, everyone.

To Tracy, Gemma and Kate: love, always.

Finally, a special vote of thanks to all the dead people who took time out from their busy schedules in the Spirit World to reveal to me, free of charge, the mysteries of Eternity: thanks guys, and see you soon!

www.ingramcontent.com/pod-product-compliance
Lightning Source LLC
Chambersburg PA
CBHW070520030426
42337CB00016B/2031